Dear Parent:
Your child's love of reading st

Every child learns to read in a different way and at his or her own speed. Some go back and forth between reading levels and read favorite books again and again. Others read through each level in order. You can help your young reader improve and become more confident by encouraging his or her own interests and abilities. From books your child reads with you to the first books he or she reads alone, there are I Can Read Books for every stage of reading:

SHARED READING
Basic language, word repetition, and whimsical illustrations, ideal for sharing with your emergent reader

BEGINNING READING
Short sentences, familiar words, and simple concepts for children eager to read on their own

READING WITH HELP
Engaging stories, longer sentences, and language play for developing readers

READING ALONE
Complex plots, challenging vocabulary, and high-interest topics for the independent reader

I Can Read Books have introduced children to the joy of reading since 1957. Featuring award-winning authors and illustrators and a fabulous cast of beloved characters, I Can Read Books set the standard for beginning readers.

A lifetime of discovery begins with the magical words **"I Can Read!"**

Visit www.icanread.com for information
on enriching your child's reading experience.

For Grandma D.
—L.D.

To the Staraselski family with
much love, x
—C.E.

I Can Read® and I Can Read Book® are trademarks of HarperCollins Publishers.
I Want to Be a Scientist
Copyright © 2024 HarperCollins
All rights reserved. Manufactured in Malaysia.
No part of this book may be used or reproduced in any manner whatsoever without written
permission except in the case of brief quotations embodied in critical articles and reviews.
For information address HarperCollins Children's Books, a division of HarperCollins Publishers,
195 Broadway, New York, NY 10007.
www.icanread.com

Library of Congress Control Number: 2023932492
ISBN 978-0-06-298965-9 (trade bdg.) — ISBN 978-0-06-298964-2 (pbk.)

23 24 25 26 27   COS   10 9 8 7 6 5 4 3 2 1
Book design by Stephanie Hays

First Edition

BEGINNING 1 READING

I Can Read!

I Want to Be a
Scientist

by Laura Driscoll
pictures by Catalina Echeverri

HARPER

An Imprint of HarperCollinsPublishers

We set sail today on a ship
headed for the North Pole!

My mom is in charge

of a team of scientists.

They record whale songs.

They take photos of their flukes.

These scientists are *marine biologists*.

Marine biologists study animals
that live in the water.
Like all scientists,
they watch, listen, and collect facts.

They test ideas

to see if they are right.

Some scientists try to find

the cause of a problem.

Some of them try to solve problems.

9

All scientists want to learn more
about our world.

There are lots of scientists on our ship.

Each one has something to study

while we are at sea.

And I get to help!

Eve studies water.

She is a *hydrologist*.

"I am testing how clean
the ocean water is," Eve says.
I help her get today's water samples.

Back on the ship,

I bring the water to Ben.

He puts it under a microscope.

"I am counting tiny life-forms in the water," Ben says.

He is a *microbiologist*.

I help Rosa with

her underwater scanner.

It is on the underside of the boat.

We control it from a computer.

"I am making a map of the sea floor,"

Rosa says.

Rosa is a *geologist*.

She studies the earth and how it changes.

Up on deck,

Jim wants to know

what the seafloor is made of.

Jim studies earthquakes—

why and where they happen.

Jim is a *seismologist*.

"Many strong earthquakes

take place underwater," Jim says.

Emma is at the weather station
on the bridge.
I help her record
the air and water temperature.

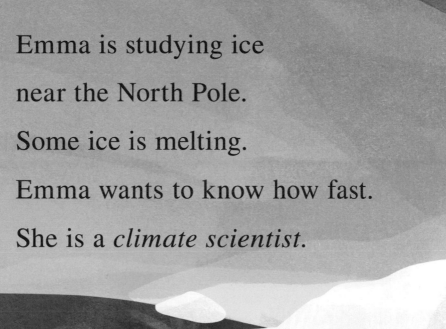

Emma is studying ice
near the North Pole.
Some ice is melting.
Emma wants to know how fast.
She is a *climate scientist*.

We go with Ty and Lena onto the ice.

Ty studies the weather.

He is a *meteorologist*.

Lena studies polar bears.

She is a *zoologist*.

Nat has come along to look into space.

The sky at sea is so clear.

He lets us look through his telescope.

He is filming a meteor shower!

Nat is an *astronomer*.

There is so much to find out
about the world!

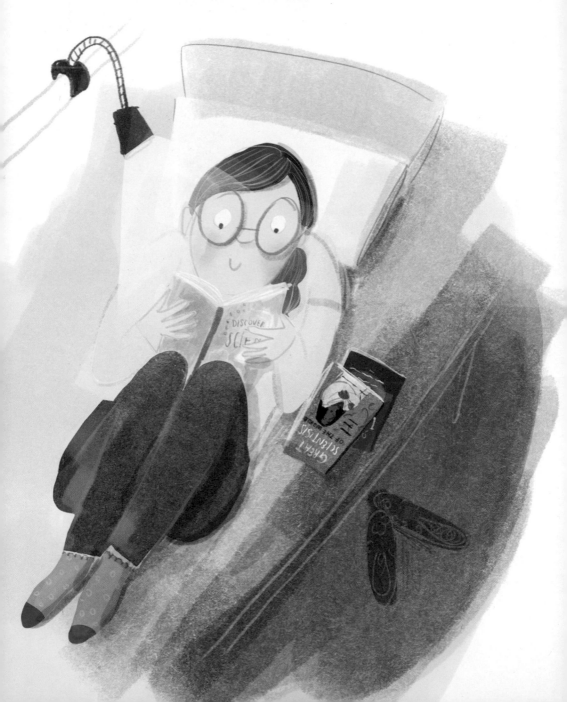

A *botanist* might ask:

What plants do bees like best?

An *epidemiologist* might ask:

What causes a disease?

A *physicist* might ask:

What is the universe made of?

Now *that* is a big question.

Maybe someday I will try to answer it.

Meet the Scientists

Marine biologist
A scientist who studies living things in the ocean

Hydrologist
A scientist who studies water: where it is, how it moves, and what is in it

Microbiologist
A scientist who wants to learn more about tiny forms of life, like bacteria

Geologist
A scientist who studies what the Earth is made of and how it has changed

Seismologist
A scientist who tracks where earthquakes happen and how strong they are

Climate scientist
Someone who studies long-term changes in Earth's temperature and weather

Meteorologist
A scientist who studies day-to-day weather

Zoologist
A scientist who tries to learn more about one or more types of animals

Astronomer
A scientist who studies space, including stars and planets

Epidemiologist
A scientist who studies diseases and how they spread

Physicist
A scientist who studies matter and energy and how they make up our universe